WHERE IS GOD?

DOES GOD DISAPPEAR WHEN YOU NEED HIM THE MOST?

BY

MICHAEL SNIDER

Where is God?

Printed in the United States of America

All Scripture quotes are from the King James Bible

ISBN: 978-1-7351454-9-5

All Scripture quotes are from the King James Bible except those verses compared and then the source is identified.

Address All Inquiries To:
THE OLD PATHS PUBLICATIONS, Inc.
142 Gold Flume Way
Cleveland, Georgia, U.S.A.

Web: www.theoldpathspublications.com
E-mail: TOP@theoldpathspublications.com

DEDICATION

Kay Snider: You are my encouraging muse.

Jonathan Snider: Never give up on your dreams.

FORWARD

John 3:16, the most famous verse in the Bible, shouts out that we matter! The proof is in the price that was paid for our salvation.

We all live with a sin nature, surrounded by people with sin natures, in a sin cursed world. Before we know it, events can spiral out of control, leaving us feeling defeated, destroyed, and desperate!

Pastor Snider challenges everyone to make the best progress out of the worst times. The Biblical truths that you need to know are in this book. It demonstrates hope for the most desperate and defeated person. No one has to stay down. No one has to stay defeated.

Pastor Snider knows what he is talking about. He points you to the Bible answers. He knows that they work.

I wish for a widespread audience for this publication.

Phil Stringer

TABLE OF CONTENTS

Introduction

And it came to pass after this, that Benhadad king of Syria gathered all his host, and went up, and besieged Samaria. And there was a great famine in Samaria: and, behold, they besieged it, until an ass's head was sold for fourscore pieces of silver, and the fourth part of a cab of dove's dung for five pieces of silver. And as the king of Israel was passing by upon the wall, there cried a woman unto him, saying, Help, my lord, O king. And he said, If the LORD do not help thee, whence shall I help thee? out of the barnfloor, or out of the winepress? And the king said unto her, What aileth thee? And she answered, This woman said unto me, Give thy son, that we may eat him to day, and we will eat my son to morrow. So we boiled my son, and did eat him: and I said unto her on the next day, Give thy son, that we may eat him: and she hath hid her son. And it came to pass, when the king heard the words of the woman, that he rent his clothes; and he passed by upon the wall, and the people looked, and, behold, he had sackcloth within upon his flesh." (2Kings 6:24-30)

Samaria found itself in a horrific situation that just went from bad to worse to nauseating. The **bad** was that Samaria was being surround by an enemy bent on their destruction. The **worse** was the besieged caused a very severe famine. Food was extremely scarce and the people were paying exorbitant prices for small amounts of anything edible. A donkey's head and dove's dung for example. The **nauseating** was when two women were so hungry, they agreed to eat each other's babies.

When one hears this story, you would have every right ask a few questions. Why did God allow this army to cause so much agony? Was God paying attention to the fact that people were suffering. Where was God?

You may ask yourself a similar question when hardship and heart break happen to you "God, where are you?"

What if it is Sunday night and you have $9.00 dollars to last you until Friday? Is God aware of your situation?

Your wife leaves you for another man and for the first time in your life you feel you have no life? Does God understand how you feel?

You lose your job and you are ashamed to go home and tell your wife. Does God care?

Maybe you have felt like Connie, "I am feeling broken. I am broken and I am weak. I am not going to lie; I have been really down. I even cried while on the road. No one knows what one goes through. Each day having to wake up wondering if it's going to be any different. A smile on my face so no one will notice my pain, yup that's me. People have said they would be there for me, but it turns out they are not."

Do you feel God is not paying attention to your dilemma? Does God seem distant from you? You seem to face tragedy after tragedy and it appears God is absolutely no help. You pray and pray and there is no answer. Ever feel that God has given up on you? So, you have given up on Him.

The world you live in is not a safe place. There are murders, wars, diseases, and tragedy. Why does God allow this to happen? You know He could step in and stop it from happening. Why does God allow suffering?

This study will ask and answer these five questions:
Is God aware of me?
Does God understand me?
Does God care?
Why do we suffer?
Where is God?

SO, THIS IS MY LIFE, A THING YOU CRUMBLE UP AND THROW TO THE FLOOR, PEOPLE STEP OVER, KICK TO THE SIDE?

THIS IS YOUR "GREAT PURPOSE" FOR MY LIFE?

OK, I ACCPECT IT.

JUST GRANT ME ONE REQUEST.

HAVE ONE PERSON SHOW ME THEY LOVE ME TODAY.

One of my actual conversations with God.

Question 1: Is God Aware of Me?

Introduction: No one wants to feel insignificant. There is no worse feeling then to be a part of a group and yet you feel invisible. It is an even worse feeling if you believe that God has somehow forgotten you exist. That He is unaware what is going on in your life.

I had such a feeling. Through a series of bad decisions and unfortunate events, I suddenly found myself homeless. I was sleeping in my Ford Escort station wagon and taking baths in a gas station bathroom. No one at my job ever knew and no one at my Church even noticed. I recall one night looking at the stars talking to God, "Do you see how I have to live? God, have you forgotten all I have done for you? This is how you treat me?" I recall rolling back and forth sobbing, "I just need a break, can someone just give me a break?"

I knew that God was not paying attention to me or worse He was ignoring my pleas for help. I did not feel important enough for God to be aware of me. I felt abounded by everyone and that included God. Was I right? Did God pay attention to more important people? Did I just not rate enough for God to notice me? Do you feel that way? God is just not aware of you and your troubles? Are you asking yourself, **"Is God aware of me?"**

The following verses will answer your question with four great truths:

"Are not two sparrows sold for a farthing? and one of them shall not fall on the grounwithout your Father. But the very hairs of your head are all numbered. Fear ye not therefore, ye are of more value than many sparrows." (Matthew 10:29-31)

Our God is aware of a small bird that falls to the ground. Nothing that happens in life is insignificant to God. He is aware of every little thing.

Nothing about you is insignificant to God. He is aware when one of your hairs falls to the ground. He is aware of every little thing about you.

NOTHING ABOUT YOU IS INSIGNIFICANT TO GOD.

*GOD KNOWS YOU AND HE VAULES YOU.

"The eyes of the LORD are in every place, beholding the evil and the good." (Proverbs 15:3)

God's eyes are everywhere. He sees every good thing and every bad thing that happens to you. God's eyes see every little thing in your life.

*GOD SEES EVERY THING THAT HAPPENS TO YOU.

"The eyes of the LORD are upon the righteous, and his ears are open unto their cry." (Psalms 34:15)

While God's eyes never stop watching you, His ears also are always open to you. He hears your every plea and listens to every fear.

*GOD HEARS YOU.

"I will be glad and rejoice in thy mercy: for thou hast considered my trouble; thou hast known my soul in adversities;" (Psalms 31:7)

God is aware of your problem and He is not ignoring you. God is aware of your every single emotion during your problem. He knows what is going on and how you feel about it.

*GOD IS PAYING ATTENTION TO YOUR PROBLEM.

No matter how busy the world gets; you are important enough for God. The God who reigns over all nations has time to deal with you one on one. **GOD IS ALWAYS AWARE OF YOU.**

You may feel lonely and abandoned, but God says you are not. He is aware of your troubles, he sees what you are going through, and He knows how you feel.

It may seem God does not listen to your prayers, but he hears you. You are not being ignored. He hears every word and he see every tear.

Hagar, an Egyptian slave of Abraham who bare him a son named Ishmael, is a great example of God's awareness.

Abraham, at the request of Sara his wife, expelled Hagar and Ishmael from the camp. Abraham only gave her and the boy some bread and water and then cast them out into the wilderness to fend for themselves. They wander in the wilderness until the bread and were spent and they were completely exhausted. Hagar and Ishmael both collapsed unto the ground and were in danger of dehydration or worse wild beast.

YOU MAY FEEL LONELY AND ABANDONED, BUT GOD SAYS YOU ARE NOT.

There they were alone, unwanted, and in distress. They could not save themselves and no one was definitely coming to rescue them. Where was God? Did He not see this? Was God aware of what was happening? Yes, He was.

"And God heard the voice of the lad; and the angel of God called to Hagar out of heaven, and said unto her, What aileth thee, Hagar? fear not; for God hath heard the voice of the lad where he is." (Genesis 21:17)

There are no greater words to the heart of the miserable: Fear not, God has heard your voice.

The tears of hopelessness were seen and the groans of misery were heard. God at that moment rescued them. For He sent an angel to open Hagar's eyes to see a well of water. She and her son were saved.

Hagar's story is encouragement for all who are suffering. **You, who are helpless and hopeless, be aware that your God is aware of you. Fear not, you who at night cry yourself to sleep, your God sees those tears and He hears those pleas.**

> *"I will lift up mine eyes unto the hills, from whence cometh my help. My help cometh from the LORD, which made heaven and earth. He will not suffer thy foot to be moved: he that keepeth thee will not slumber. Behold, he that keepeth Israel shall neither slumber nor sleep. The LORD is thy keeper: the LORD is thy shade upon thy right hand. The sun shall not smite thee by day, nor the moon by night. The LORD shall preserve thee from all evil: he shall preserve thy soul. The LORD shall preserve thy going out and thy coming in from this time forth, and even for evermore." (Psalm 121:1-8)*

YOUR GOD ALWAYS WATCHES OVER YOU.

Conclusion

The morning after the night of my tearful questioning of God, He revealed to me He was paying attention. I had finished my bath in the gas station bathroom and was in line to pay for my breakfast. I overheard a conversation between two men ahead of me in line. The one man told the other that a trailer park near me that I was familiar with rented cheap trailers. The other man stated that that he did not know that and I commented to myself, "neither did I".

Later that day after I got off work, I drove straight to the trailer park to inquire about the cheap trailers for rent. I knocked on the door of the office not knowing what to expect. Nothing could have prepared for who answered the door. I was surprised to find out that I knew the owner from my church circles I was involved in. I explained to him my situation and that I had no money at the moment, but I did have a job. He told me that not only would he rent me a trailer but he would not charge me a deposit. He stated that Christian brothers are to help each other out. That night I had a place to sleep. There were no lights, no bed, and no heat, but I had a place to sleep.

God had seen and heard me. He had sent me to the right place and to the right person for my help and I had learned a valuable lesson. God is aware of me and my situations. He does not forget about me. God does not forget about you.

GOD YOU KNOW I HAVE LOST EVERYTHING.

DOES THAT NOT EVEN MATTER TO YOU?

HOW MANY MORE TEARS DO YOU WANT FROM ME?

One of my actual conversations with God.

Question 2: Does God Understand Me?

Introduction

Just to have someone who understands how you feel is a comforting feeling. Someone who understands where you are coming from is a calming presence. Unfortunately, there are many situations where we face problems so alone that no one even can relate to us. Have you not spent time alone in a quiet place wanting someone to talk to, but no one will or wants to hear you? I know I have. And the loneliness just adds to the pain.

It was just a few months removed from when my wife left me and everyone else had moved on. There were someone else's problems to talk about, to care about. So, when I did get the occasional, "How are you holding up?" I would just answer, "OK" even when I were not. No one would truly understand how I felt. No one wanted to take the time to even try to understand how I felt.

I put up a good front around people at work or church, because that is what they wanted from me. But I would go home every night after work or church and crawl into my bed or couch, wrap myself around my pillow, and just cry and cry.

I even doubted that God understood my feelings at that time, because if He did, why was He allowing all this pain and confusion to cripple me? Why does He not reach down and take it all away? I even told Him once,

"God, I am not ok here." How could God possibly understand any of this?

The following verses assisted me with my doubts with four reassuring truths:

> *"O LORD, thou hast searched me, and known me. Thou knowest my downsitting and mine uprising, thou understandest my thought afar off. Thou compassest my path and my lying down, and art acquainted with all my ways. For there is not a word in my tongue, but, lo, O LORD, thou knowest it altogether." (Psalm 139:1-4)*

God knows when you sit down. God knows when you sit up. God knows where you are going. God knows where you sleep. God knows your future thoughts. God knows why you say what you say. There is nothing that God does not know about you.

*GOD KNOWS YOU PERSONALLY.

> *"And thou, Solomon my son, know thou the God of thy father, and serve him with a perfect heart and with a willing mind: for the LORD searcheth all hearts, and understandeth all the imaginations of the thoughts: if thou seek him, he will be found of thee; but if thou forsake him, he will cast thee off for ever." (1Chronicles 28:9)*

Not one of your emotions slips pass God. He knows how you feel about all that touches your life. God knows your every thought on every subject in your life. He knows what motivates your thinking.

*GOD KNOWS HOW YOU THINK.

"But the LORD said unto Samuel, Look not on his countenance, or on the height of his stature; because I have refused him: for the LORD seeth not as man seeth; for man looketh on the outward appearance, but the LORD looketh on the heart." (1Samuel 16:7)

God knows you beyond what is seen by others. God knows your very center of who you are. He knows you are more then what you allow the world to see of you.

*GOD KNOWS THE REAL YOU.

"Before I formed thee in the belly I knew thee; and before thou camest forth out of the womb I sanctified thee, and I ordained thee a prophet unto the nations." (Jeremiah 1:5)

God knew you before you even existed. He knew when you would be conceived and ang He was involved in each stage of your fetal development.

GOD KNOWS EXACTLY THE REASON FOR YOUR EVERY JOY AND YOUR EVERY SORROW.

*GOD KNEW YOU BEFORE YOU WERE YOU.

You have never told anyone, but you have hopes and dreams that have never come true. God understands how that has broken your heart.

Deep in your soul there are secrets regrets that not even your closes friends know about. Yet, God knows how you wrestle with your guilt.

God knows exactly the reason for your every joy and your every sorrow. When it comes to you, nothing catches God by surprise. **GOD UNDERSTANDS EVERYTHING ABOUT YOU.** Jesus compares His understanding of you like a shepherd of his sheep.

> *"I am the good shepherd, and know my sheep, and am known of mine." (John 10:14)*

> *"My sheep hear my voice, and I know them, and they follow me:" (John 10:27)*

Jesus is like a good shepherd who spends so much of his time with his sheep that he knows every little thing about them. Nothing gets pass your Good Shepherd. Just like a good shepherd, Jesus knows his sheep. He knows who you are, where you are going, and why you do what you do. He knows what you can and cannot do. He knows what you need and do not need. God knows the real you not the false face you show others. The Good Shepherd knows you as if you were His only sheep.

> *"For he is our God; and we are the people of his pasture, and the sheep of his hand. To day if ye will hear his voice," (Psalm 95:7)*

You are the sheep of God's provision and of His strength. That means God will provide what you hunger for and deliver you from what troubles you, if you listen to your Good Shepherd. Those who will not listen to the Good Shepherd are empty and in danger.

GOD KNOWS YOU SO WELL THAT HE THINKS ABOUT YOU.

His thoughts for you are a better end then all this evil around you. You are safe in the mind of God.

> *"For I know the thoughts that I think toward you, saith the LORD, thoughts of peace, and not of evil, to give you an expected end." (Jerimiah 29:11)*

The wonder of God is not only does He know you, but His thoughts dwell on you.

Conclusion

What about you? Are you putting on the brave face because that is what others want from you? I know I was. There was not one person who understood me. I even

NO ONE KNOWS ME BETTER THAN MY GOD.

had myself convince that God could not even relate to my pain. How could He possibly know what it feels like to be betrayed and made a fool? What does God know about lose? God does not know what it means to struggle in this life. How foolish I was.

> *"For verily he took not on him the nature of angels; but he took on him the seed of Abraham. Wherefore in all things it behoved him to be made like unto his brethren, that he might be a merciful and faithful high priest in things pertaining to God, to make reconciliation for the sins of the people. For in that he himself hath suffered being tempted, he is able to succour them that are tempted." (Hebrews 2:16-18)*

> *"For we have not an high priest which cannot be touched with the feeling of our infirmities; but was in all points tempted like as we are, yet without sin." (Hebrews 4:15)*

During a sermon from a TV preacher, which I hardly ever watch, God reminded me that He once lived among us and He does understand how it feels to struggle in this live. Jesus did suffer heartache and He did know what it felt like to be betrayed. Jesus can relate to the pain from losing everything. He even lost His life. So how foolish of me to criticize God for not understanding me. No one knows me better than my God.

Question 3: Does God Care?

Introduction

No one cares. I mean people talk a big game. "Let me know if you need anything", they say, but when you ask for help – nothing. People are not getting directly involved If things do not directly involve them. They do not mind talking with others about your pain and they enjoy telling you what went wrong to put you in the misery, but to care enough to help? No.

I recall a horrible night that I was in a bad way with my Crohn's Disease. I was in immense pain, so much so I groaned and moaned the entire night. I laid on the floor at the foot bed with a bucket next to me because my stomach was so upset. My fever was so merciless that the sweat kept my clothes wet. I have never felt that close to my own death. The worse of the whole ordeal was the entire night I lay there suffering not one person cared enough to check on me. Not one single person cared. I mean at this point, did God even care?

The following verses answered my suspicions of God's concern for me with six incredible truths:

> *"Thou tellest my wanderings: put thou my tears into thy bottle: are they not in thy book?" (Psalm 56:8)*

God can describe your every lost moment. He knows when you have no clue where you are going in life or what you are doing.

*GOD CARES WHEN YOU ARE CONFUSED.

God can describe your every tear. He records your tears not one of them is forgotten by Him.

*GOD CARES ABOUT YOUR EVERY TEAR.

"In all their affliction he was afflicted, and the angel of his presence saved them: in his love and in his pity he redeemed them; and he bare them, and carried them all the days of old." (Isaiah 63:9)

God feels your suffering. Your pain is very real to God, because it is His pain also. When you hurt, God hurts.

*GOD CARES WHEN YOU ARE HURTING.

"When I cry unto thee, then shall mine enemies turn back: this I know; for God is for me." (Psalm 56:9)

God is for you. When others are against you, God stands with you.

*GOD CARES WHEN OTHERS ARE AGAINST YOU.

"Casting all your care upon him; for he careth for you." (1Peter 5:7)

God wants your concerns. God wants you to share with him all your fears and worries, because He cares for you. If it bothers you, it bothers God.

*GOD CARES ABOUT YOUR TROUBLES.

> *"Now the God of hope fill you with all joy and peace in believing, that ye may abound in hope, through the power of the Holy Ghost." (Romans 15:13)*

God is the God of hope. When you trust God, He brings to you an overflow of hope. Hope that never ends.

*GOD'S CARE FILLS YOU WITH HIS HOPE.

If you have had moments of doubts about God's caring for you, do not worry you are not the only one. Even the Disciples had their moment of doubt.

> *"And there arose a great storm of wind, and the waves beat into the ship, so that it was now full. And he was in the hinder part of the ship, asleep on a pillow: and they awake him, and say unto him, Master, carest thou not that we perish?" (Mark 4:37-38)*

Storms will arise in your life and you will feel all alone. You pray and beg God for help, yet no answer. You cannot see that God is involved at all. It is like He has fallen asleep on you. "God are you there? Do you care?" are natural questions in moments like these.

You are tired from the sleepless nights. You toss and turn with constant thoughts on your circumstances. Possibly, you feel like Joe, "I haven't felt like this in a long time, but's 4:30 in the morning. Woke up and it just feels like today is harder than yesterday. Man!"

Your problems become such a burden that they truly keep you from living life. You beg yourself to stop crying and be strong, but you are not strong. You are barely functioning for your thoughts are constantly on your deep pain. You know something needs to change or you will die. "God do you care?" Yet, in the middle of your emotional storm, if you listen, you will hear Jesus say, "Peace, be still." (Mark 4:39) When you obey this simple command you will experiences a great calm in your soul that not even you can explain. **GOD IS CONCERNED ABOUT YOU**.

DOES GOD CARE? YES, HE CARES. In times of trouble God provides for you:

REST

"Come unto me, all ye that labour and are heavy laden, and i will give you rest." (Mathew 11:28)

ENCOURAGEMENT

"Who comforteth us in all our tribulation, that we may be able to comfort them which are in any trouble, by the comfort wherewith we ourselves are comforted of God." (2 Corinthians 1:4)

JOY

"Now the God of hope fill you with all joy and peace in believing, that ye may abound in hope, through the power of the Holy Ghost." (Romans 15:13)

PEACE

"Now the God of hope fill you with all joy and peace in believing, that ye may abound in hope, through the power of the Holy Ghost." (Romans 15:13)

ENDURANCE

"There hath no temptation taken you but such as is common to man: but God is faithful, who will not suffer you to be tempted above that ye are able; but will with the temptation also make a way to escape, that ye may be able to bear it." (1 Corinthians 10:13)

DIRECTION

"There hath no temptation taken you but such as is common to man: but God is faithful, who will not suffer you to be tempted above that ye are able; but will with the temptation also make a way to escape, that ye may be able to bear it." (1 Corinthians 10:13)

Conclusion

Morning did come, and I had not died. The house was empty, and I was alone. I was still so sick, and I did not know if I had any sleep. I changed into a pair of blue jeans and t-shirt and struggled to put my shoes on. I was going to Doctor even if I did not have an appointment. I drove to the went to the Doctor's office and to this day I do not know how I got there. The doctor agreed to see me and laid down on one of the couches and fell asleep. Nurse woke me up and I managed to make it to the right room. And once again I just lay there.

When the doctor arrived, I relived that horrible night to him. The doctor shook his head and said, "you had quite a night." He ran some tests and took some x-rays. He then gave me some pain medicine and told me to go home and get some rest.

GOD WILL ALWAYS BE THERE AS A FAITHFUL, CARING FRIEND.

Instead of rest, I went home and begin to mow the lawn. I did not get more than half done, when there was a yell of my name. I had a phone call from the doctor that instructed me to go straight to the hospital. I needed surgery and right now.

I did as I was told and not long after arriving to the hospital, I found myself in prep for surgery. I was told I had been pushed to front of the line and will being in surgery very early in the morning.

During the hospital check in process I was asked if I had a pastor at that time, I was the pastor, but I did mention my pastor I worked for as a youth pastor years ago. He moved to Florida and I moved some place in Indiana

I did not know then just how much that insignificant answer would end up meaning the world to me. I am not sure how long the surgery took, but when I came too, he was there beside my bed. I had not seen him for years, yet there he was. He had no obligation to be there. I had not asked for him to be there. He had drove the time it took to get to my hospital and was there in time for me to come too. Why? Because he was concerned for me. Someone did care! People do care.

How much does our God care for us? Would he not travel the universe to care for one of his own? My friend never doubt your God cares for you. He is there for you no matter where you are, no matter the circumstance, He cares for you. God will always be there as a faithful, caring friend.

GOD, WHAT AWFUL THING HAVE I DONE TO DESERVE THIS?

WHAT MAKES ME SO BAD?

WHY DO I NOT DESERVE TO BE HAPPY LIKE EVERYONE ELSE?

One of my actual conversations with God.

Question 4: Why Do We Suffer?

Introduction

Why would a Christian experience the hurts and troubles of this life? I mean with God as our Father, Protector, Helper, and Savior, how could anything possibility go wrong? Yet, we all know things do go wrong, sometimes horrible wrong. Many Christians struggle with their relationship with God and with others, because they cannot come to terms with the fact that things in their life are not perfect. Which begs the question – **WHY DO WE SUFFER?**

> *"Beloved, think it not strange concerning the fiery trial which is to try you, as though some strange thing happened unto you: But rejoice, inasmuch as ye are partakers of Christ's sufferings; that, when his glory shall be revealed, ye may be glad also with exceeding joy. If ye be reproached for the name of Christ, happy are ye; for the spirit of glory and of God resteth upon you: on their part he is evil spoken of, but on your part he is glorified. But let none of you suffer as a murderer, or as a thief, or as an evildoer, or as a busybody in other men's matters. Yet if any man suffer as a Christian, let him not be ashamed; but let him glorify God on this behalf. For the time is come that judgment must begin at the house of God: and if it first begin at us, what shall the end be of them that obey not the gospel of God? And if the righteous scarcely be saved, where shall the ungodly and the sinner appear? Wherefore let them that suffer according to the will of God commit the keeping of their souls to him in well*

doing, as unto a faithful Creator." (1Peter 4:12-19)

Christians suffer because it is the natural part of everyday life.

12 "Beloved, think it not strange concerning the fiery trial which is to try you, as though some strange thing happened unto you:" (1 Peter 4:12)

Life is difficult. Wow is that an understatement. The harsh reality of life is that without warning unforeseen hardships occur. A car accident, A broken appliance, or a Sick child just happens whether you are prepared for it or not. Who has not had a day when the boss is in a bad mood, or the spouse wants to argue, or you just said something stupid? Bottom line, life is messy, and things just happen.

Paul explains to us that we should not think it stranger (foreign, odd) when fiery (passionate, emotional) problems occur in our lives. The troubles of life happen naturally unto all mankind. The righteous and the unrighteous unlike suffer from the troubles that come from the grind everyday life.

"Man that is born of a woman is of few days, and full of trouble." (Job 14:1)

Therefore, Christian, one reason you suffer is because it is natural for every living being to have troubles. Your Christianity does not make you immune from misfortunes that come from being alive.

Christians suffer for the cause of Christ. Just because you are a Christian.

> *[14] "If ye be reproached for the name of Christ, [16] Yet if any man suffer as a Christian," (1 Peter 4:14)*

I wish it were not true, but there are times you will be harmed for the simple fact you are a Christians. They are several people or groups of people who hate Jesus (even His name) and do go out of their way to mistreat or destroy his followers. Again, we should not be surprise of this hatred, Jesus did warn us that it will happen.

> *"If the world hate you, ye know that it hated me before it hated you. [19] If ye were of the world, the world would love his own: but because ye are not of the world, but I chosen you out of the world, therefore the world hateth you. (John 15:18,19)*

According to verses fourteen and sixteen of 1 Peter 4, there are two types of troubles that come to a Christian, just for being a Christian: 1. **Reproach** 2. **Suffer**

Reproach – criticism, scolding, blame, and disapproval. *[14] If you are reproached for the name of Christ,*

Suffer – distress, misery, afflict, torment, harm *[16] Yet if anyone suffers as a Christian,*

Yes, throughout history Christians have been oppressed, tortured, and even killed for who they are. Even today there are many places in our world where it is not safe to be known as a Christian. Governments, religions, and hate groups harass Christians to keep them quite, they torture Christians to change their behavior, and they kill Christians to prohibit the multiplying of their faith. Once again, we should not be surprise by this, Jesus did warn us that is what would happen.

> *"Remember the word that I said unto you, The servant is not greater than his lord. If they have persecuted me, they will also persecute you; if they have kept my saying, they will keep yours also." (John 15:20)*

Maybe you do not fear for your life where you live, but you do fear for your daily living. Christians have been harassed at work, groups, and organizations in hopes that we will conform to society's will. Those who have not conformed have lost jobs, positions, and allegiance from family and friends.

Christians suffer because of their sin. (evil doing)

> *15 But let none of you suffer as a murderer, or as a thief, or as an evildoer, or as a busybody in other men's matters. (1 Peter 4:15)*

When we sin as a Christian God deals with us in one of two ways, either His punishment or His goodness (grace) and both ways is to bring us to repentance (amends, change). But we always suffer the consequences of our sin.

The grace that God displays to a Christian that has sinned is not a subject that many speak about, but it is a startling truth. God sometimes chooses to be patient, tolerant, and kind to the sinning Christian. His grace thrives where our sin thrives.

> *" ... But where sin abounded, grace did much more abound..." (Romans 5:20)*

For many reasons, a Christian cannot use the grace of God as an excuse to continue in their sin.

> *Romans 6:1-2 "What shall we say then? Shall we continue in sin, that grace may abound? God forbid. How shall we, that are dead to sin, live any longer therein?" (Romans 6:1-2)*

So now the question, why does a holy God, who hates sin, sometimes chooses to be kind, patient, and tolerant toward the sinning Christians? The answer is simply. He wants His grace that He places upon us to convince us to repent. His goodness is shown instead of correction to move our hearts into repentance. Your love of God should have you question, "How can I treat God so horribly, while He is so good to me?"

> *"Or despisest thou the riches of his goodness and forbearance, and longsuffering, not knowing that the goodness of God leadeth thee to repentance?" (Romans 2:4)*

More often than not the sinning Christian suffers from the caring hand of God. God's discipline comes in four different forms: Correction, Chastened, Rebuke, and Scourges.

> *"Behold, happy is the man whom God* ***correcteth****; Therefore despise not thou the* ***chastening*** *of the Almighty. For he maketh sore, and bindeth up; he woundeth, and his hands make whole. (Job 5:17-18)*

> *"And ye have forgotten the exhortation which speaketh unto you as unto children: My son, despise not thou the* ***chastening*** *of the LORD, Nor faint when thou art* ***rebuked*** *of him; For whom the LORD loveth He chasteneth, And* ***scourgeth*** *every son whom he receiveth. If ye endure chastening, God dealeth with you as with sons; for what son is he whom the father chasteneth not?" (Hebrews 12:5-7)*

Correction: God's opportunity for you to make things right.

Chastened: God's attempt to humble you.

Rebuke: God criticizing you. God's scolding of you. (Bible, Preaching)

Scourges: God's inflicts pain. He becomes a curse to you.

When you become a Christian your relationship with God changes. No longer is God your judge instead, God becomes your father and you are His child. These four forms of discipline are not unlike that those performed by any other good parent.

Each time God disciplines His child it is His endeavor for that Christian to repent of their sin. He cares for us and it is His hope for every Christian to live the best possible life. Being God, he understands the damage and burden sin brings upon us. The suffering he brings into our lives is much less pain then the miserable existence our sin brings upon us.

> *"For My **yoke** is easy and My **burden** is light." (Matthew 11:30)*

Christians suffer because it is the will of God.

> *[19] "Wherefore let them that suffer according to the will of God" (1 Peter 4:19)*

I must admit even I struggle with the concept that God will determine I should suffer. That He will intentionally bring pain into my life for His purpose. But that is exactly what God does, He improves us by trying us.

Suffering and the Will of God

1. God had decided that every believer will suffer.

> *"For unto you it is given in the behalf of Christ, not only to believe on him, but also to suffer for his sake," (Philippians 1:29)*

2. God's testing of a Christian's faith is to strengthen their resolve. We cannot allow the sorrow from our burden to overcome us and weaken our faith in God. Yes, He does know what is happening, Yes, He does care, and No, He has not forgotten you.

"My brethren, count it all joy when ye fall into divers temptations, knowing this that the trying of your faith worketh patience." (James 1:2-3)

3. The Christian's genuine faith during suffering is to produce Praise, Honor, and Glory.

*"Wherein ye greatly rejoice, though now for a season, if need be, ye are in heavinesss through manifold temptations: that the **trial** of your faith, being much more precious than of gold that perisheth, though it be tried with fire, might be found unto **praise and honor and glory** at the appearing of Jesus Christ," (1 Peter 1:6-7)*

When Christians Do Suffer Paul reminds Us:

"We are troubled on every side, yet not distressed; we are perplexed, but not in despair; Persecuted, but not forsaken; cast down, but not destroyed." (2Corinthians 4:8-9)

We are troubled: We are hard-pressed (pressured, stressed) on every side.

- ***But not crushed.***

We are perplexed: (confused, stunned)

- ***But not in despair. (hopeless)***

We are persecuted: (wronged, offended, harassed)

- ***But not forsaken.***

We are struck down: (pushed down, demoted, made lower)

- ***But not destroyed.***

Conclusion

Why do Christians suffer? Because it is necessary. Suffering necessary to strengthen us. Think of it like a football player. A good coach makes practice is difficult, some may even say he causes his players unnecessary pain. When you play the game the team that has the strength to endure to the end usually wins. The same thing with life. Suffering is necessary to strengthen us. The pain you are going through right now can build you or crush you. Determine to allow it to build you.

What Suffering Strengthens in You:

- ✔ Obedience
- ✔ Endurance
- ✔ Faith
- ✔ Relationships

- ✔ Humility
- ✔ Compassion
- ✔ Commitment

That is why Christians are told to count it all joy.

"My brethren, count it all joy when ye fall into divers temptations" (James 1:2)

APPARENTLY, GOD YOU LIKE ME BROKEN AND ALONE.

WHY WILL YOU NOT FIX THIS?

One of my actual conversations with God.

Question 5: Where Is God?

Introduction

One-night despair woke me and had me trapped in my bed. I looked into the dark face of my anxieties and I trembled as I placed my head in my hands. My fears whispered to me, "Where is your God now?" I found myself praying repeating that same question, "God where are you in all of this? God, where are you?" I felt alone, afraid, and helpless.

Where is God during times of turmoil? Has He left us on our own to fend for ourselves? I know people say, "God will not allow more on you then you can handle." But I know for a fact that is not true. God has regularly allowed tragedies into my life I have no strength to endure. I pray and I pray and nothing happens. If He want to, God could stop all of this pain; He could heal this situation; He could rescue me, but He is nowhere to be found.

The following story aided me in understanding my question, "Where was God in all of this?"

> *"Now a certain man was sick, named Lazarus, of Bethany, the town of Mary and her sister Martha. (It was that Mary which anointed the Lord with ointment, and wiped his feet with her hair, whose brother Lazarus was sick.) Therefore his sisters sent unto him, saying, Lord, behold, he whom thou lovest is sick. When Jesus heard that, he said, This sickness is not unto death, but for the glory of God, that the Son of God might be glorified thereby. Now Jesus loved Martha, and*

her sister, and Lazarus. When he had heard therefore that he was sick, he abode two days still in the same place where he was." (John 11:1-6)

What do we know so far in this story?

- **There was a real problem.** This man's sickness was serious enough to his sisters they feared his death was probable.
- **Request for help was made.** His sisters knew if they sent their request for help to Jesus, He would heal their brother. Jesus has healed so many others. They placed their faith in Jesus.
- **Jesus did nothing.** Jesus knew the sister's prayers and He ignored them. Jesus did absolutely nothing to assist them.

"Then after that saith he to his disciples, Let us go into Judaea again." (John 11:7)

"Then said Jesus unto them plainly, Lazarus is dead." (John 11:14)

What more do we know in this story?

- **Jesus does something.** After a two-day delay, Jesus finally decides to response to the sisters' request for help.
- **Jesus knows the man is dead.** He waited two days knowing that the bother would die. Jesus never intended on stopping the man's death.

The response to Jesus when He finally arrives.

"Then said Martha unto Jesus, Lord, if thou hadst been here, my brother had not died." (John 11:21)

"And whosoever liveth and believeth in me shall never die. Believest thou this?" (John 11:26)

- **Martha:** Jesus, where were you?
- **Jesus:** Martha, do you trust me?

"Then when Mary was come where Jesus was, and saw him, she fell down at his feet, saying unto him, Lord, if thou hadst been here, my brother had not died." (John 11:32)

"And some of them said, Could not this man, which opened the eyes of the blind, have caused that even this man should not have died?" (John 11:37)

- **Mary:** Jesus, where were you?
- **Some in the crowd:** Jesus, where were you?

"Jesus said, Take ye away the stone. Martha, the sister of him that was dead, saith unto him, Lord, by this time he stinketh: for he hath been dead four days." (John 11:39)

"Jesus saith unto her, Said I not unto thee, that, if thou wouldest believe, thou shouldest see the glory of God?" (John 11:40)

- **Jesus:** Open the grave.

- **Martha:** Jesus you are to late. You did nothing and now there is nothing for you to do.
- **Jesus:** Martha, do you trust me?

Let us examine what we know so far in the story.

1. A man becomes gravely sick and his sisters ask Jesus for help.
2. Jesus delays thus allow the man to die. The sisters' request goes unanswered.
3. Jesus is asked several times, "Where were you?"
4. Jesus' only answer was, "Do you trust me?"

The lesson here is that God does the same to us. We pray and beg Him for a solution to our problem with no answer insight. Many times, the very thing we ask deliverance from happens to us. However, the entire time God is asking us, **"DO YOU TRUST ME?"** My friends the answer to that question is everything. When it feels God is nowhere to be found, like He is not listening at all to your request, **DO YOU TRUST HIM?**

When God asks that question to you, it is not like it is truly a blind trust. We already have seen that God is aware of you, that He understands you, and that He cares about you. You know that are reasons why you suffer. But there is another reason you can trust God when it seems He is absent in your hour of greatest need. Let look deeper into John chapter eleven and see the four reason Jesus gives for trusting Him.

> *"When Jesus heard that, he said, This sickness is not unto death, but for the glory of God, that the*

> *Son of God might be glorified thereby." (John 11:4)*

*JESUS MADE A PROMISE.

Jesus asked to be trusted because He promised, "This is not unto death." God will ask you to trust Him because he promises you:

> *"Fear thou not; for I am with thee: be not dismayed; for I am thy God: I will strengthen thee; yea, I will help thee; yea, I will uphold thee with the right hand of my righteousness." (Isiah 41:10)*

Do you trust Him?

> *"Now Jesus loved Martha, and her sister, and Lazarus." (John 11:5)*

*JESUS LOVED THEM.

Jesus asked to be trusted because He loved them. God will ask you to trust him because He loves you.

> *"The LORD hath appeared of old unto me, saying, Yea, I have loved thee with an everlasting love: therefore with lovingkindness have I drawn thee." (Jeremiah 31:3)*

Do you trust Him?

> *"Jesus wept." (John 11:35)*

*JESUS HAD COMPASSION.

Jesus asked to be trusted because He had compassion on those near Him. God will ask you to trust Him because of His compassion for you.

> *"Blessed be God, even the Father of our Lord Jesus Christ, the Father of mercies, and the God of all comfort; Who comforteth us in all our tribulation, that we may be able to comfort them which are in any trouble, by the comfort wherewith we ourselves are comforted of God." (2Corinthians 1:3-4)*

Do you trust Him?

> *"When Jesus heard that, he said, This sickness is not unto death, but for the glory of God, that the Son of God might be glorified thereby." (John 11:4)*

> *"Jesus saith unto her, Said I not unto thee, that, if thou wouldest believe, thou shouldest see the glory of God?" (John 11:40)*

*JESUS HAD A PLAN AND A PURPOSE.

Jesus asked to be trusted because He had plan and purpose for the man's death. God will ask you to trust Him because of His plan and purpose for you.

> *"In whom also we have obtained an inheritance, being predestinated according to the purpose of him who worketh all things after the counsel of his own will: That we should be to the praise of his*

glory, who first trusted in Christ." (Ephesians 1:11-12

Do you trust Him?

Conclusion

In the story of John eleven, Jesus made it no secret what His plan was and the purpose for that plan. Jesus' plan was to allow the man to die and yes, his sisters would have to experience the awful pain from losing him. Jesus also did not hide the purpose of His plan.

> *"And I am glad for your sakes that I was not there, to the intent ye may believe; nevertheless let us go unto him." (John 11:15)*

Jesus told his disciples that this situation was to bring them and others to trust in God and that is exactly what happen.

> *"And he that was dead came forth, bound hand and foot with graveclothes: and his face was bound about with a napkin. Jesus saith unto them, Loose him, and let him go. Then many of the Jews which came to Mary, and had seen the things which Jesus did, believed on him." (John 11:44-45)*

To the astonishment of everyone, Jesus rose Lazarus from the dead. That one amazing miracle created trust in Jesus not only in that day but for those of us who read this story today.

STOP BEING A VICTIM OF YOUR CIRCUMSTANCES AND ACCEPT THE PLAN AND PURPOSE OF GOD.

Can you imagine how the joy that filled his sisters' heart to once again hold their brother in their arms. When Jesus was allowed to execute His plan and His purpose was revealed, Lazarus, Mary, and Martha were no longer victims.

Here lies they lesson: Where was Jesus in this story? He was all in it from begging to end. Many asked him where He was not once thinking that Jesus had a plan and purpose for all of this.

Friend bad things will happen to you. You will pray and pray and it seems God is nowhere to be found. But do not despair - He is all into your situation. He has a plan and a purpose for you troubles. **When you accept that God has a plan and purpose for your suffering you are no longer a victim.** With that acceptance comes peace and empowerment. Do you trust God? Do you trust that He has your best interest at heart? He has a plan and purpose for you. Stop being a victim of your circumstances and accept the plan and purpose of God.

I have been asked several times in my life, "With all you have been through in your life, why are you still happy, still confident." The answer is easy. Even though things bring me pain, even though I am afraid, and even if I lose everything. I know God has this. He loves me and He cares for me. I accept His plan and His purpose and refuse to be a victim; I chose to allow God to be glorified in my situation. He has always been there; I no longer ask God where He is, because I know He is all in this. I trust Him to do right by me.

God reaches out His hand and whispers, "I am here, do you trust me?"

> *"For the scripture saith, Whosoever believeth on him shall not be ashamed." (Romans 10:11)*

CONCLUSION:

> *"And there were four leprous men at the entering in of the gate: and they said one to another, Why sit we here until we die? If we say, We will enter into the city, then the famine is in the city, and we shall die there: and if we sit still here, we die also. Now therefore come, and let us fall unto the host of the Syrians: if they save us alive, we shall live; and if they kill us, we shall but die. And they rose up in the twilight, to go unto the camp of the Syrians: and when they were come to the uttermost part of the camp of Syria, behold, there was no man there. For the Lord had made the host of the Syrians to hear a noise of chariots, and a noise of horses, even the noise of a great host: and they said one to another, Lo, the king of Israel hath hired against us the kings of the Hittites, and the kings of the Egyptians, to come upon us. Wherefore they arose and fled in the twilight, and left their tents, and their horses, and their asses,*

> *even the camp as it was, and fled for their life. And when these lepers came to the uttermost part of the camp, they went into one tent, and did eat and drink, and carried thence silver, and gold, and raiment, and went and hid it; and came again, and entered into another tent, and carried thence also, and went and hid it." (2Kings 7:3-8)*

Let us return to the horrible situation in Samaria. Four hopeless leper men, who believed that they were on their own, decided they were out of options. No matter what answer they chose to solve their terrible situation, they were going to die. Have you ever been there? You have no right answers. No matter what you do, it is bad.

These lepers decided to give up and hope for mercy from their oppressors, but instead of mercy, they found the providence of God. Unknowingly God had already removed the crisis. At the very moment it was needed when it was the best, God moved. The sad thing is all the foolishness, worrying, and evil acts in Samaria did not have to happen. For God performs in the right moment, not too early and not too late, but right on time.

You hate not knowing the future. You want to know what is the next step in your life. And during trying times, you fear not knowing the future. You are desperate to know when, how, or if God is going to rescue you.

If you are like me, waiting on God is frustrating, but wait you must. For God's moment is not here, but if you remain faithful, your challenge will have a God moment.

- **HE IS THE GOD OF THE MOMENT!**

"Then spake Elisha unto the woman, whose son he had restored to life, saying, Arise, and go thou and thine household, and sojourn wheresoever thou canst sojourn: for the LORD hath called for a famine; and it shall also come upon the land seven years. And the woman arose, and did after the saying of the man of God: and she went with her household, and sojourned in the land of the Philistines seven years." (2 Kings 8:1-2)

- **THERE WAS TROUBLE: FAMINE**

"And it came to pass at the seven years' end, that the woman returned out of the land of the Philistines: and she went forth to cry unto the king for her house and for her land." (2 Kings 8:3)

- **THERE WAS LOSS: HOUSE AND LAND**

"And the king talked with Gehazi the servant of the man of God, saying, Tell me, I pray thee, all the great things that Elisha hath done. And it came to pass, as he was telling the king how he had restored a dead body to life, that, behold, the woman, whose son he had restored to life, cried to the king for her house and for her land. And Gehazi said, My lord, O king, this is the woman, and this is her son, whom Elisha restored to life. And when the king asked the woman, she told him. So the king appointed unto her a certain officer, saying, Restore all that was hers, and all

the fruits of the field since the day that she left the land, even until now." (2Kings 8:4-6)

• THERE WAS THE GOD OF THE MOMENT: RESTORED ALL THAT WAS HERS

God knows that exact moment when to act. He will has not forgotten you and He is paying attention to what is going on in your life. Trust him and wait for His moment. Waiting is not always easy, but if you wait, God will have His moment.

WAIT ON GOD!

God has not left you to face your troubles on your own. While God is not Santa Clause giving you whatever you ask for, He will rescue you. God even became human to rescue all of mankind from the violence of their sin. Therefore, He will not allow you to be destroyed. He will not forsake you. He understands your suffering, how you feel, and how desperate things are for you. You are very important to Him. Luke 12 records Jesus describing to you how important you are to God.

"Consider the ravens: for they neither sow nor reap; which neither have storehouse nor barn; and God feedeth them: how much more are ye better than the fowls?" (Luke 12:24)

The God who cares for the wellbeing of the fowls of this world cares more about you. He knows what is going on in your life and He has a plan for it. So, wait for God's moment for your life.

WAIT ON GOD AND HE WILL STRENGTHEN YOU.

"But they that wait upon the LORD shall renew their strength; they shall mount up with wings as eagles; they shall run, and not be weary; and they shall walk, and not faint." (Isaiah 40:31)

RENEWED STRENGTH:

- **STRENGTH TO RISE ABOUT IT ALL**
- **STRENGTH TO ADVANCE AND NOT BE DISHEARTENED.**
- **STRENGTH TO MAKE IMPROVEMENTS AND NOT QUIT**

WAIT ON GOD AND HE WILL BLESS YOU

"And therefore will the LORD wait, that he may be gracious unto you, and therefore will he be exalted, that he may have mercy upon you: for the LORD is a God of judgment: blessed are all they that wait for him." (Isaiah 30:18)

- **BLESS YOU WITH HIS FAVOR**
- **BLESS YOU WITH HIS COMPASSION**
- **BLESS YOU WITH HIS JUSTICE**

WAIT ON YOUR GOD:

- God is aware of you, wait on Him.
- God understands you, wait on His understanding.
- God cares for you, wait on that caring.
- God has a reason for your suffering, wait on that reason.
- God is always where He is supposed to be, wait on His plan and purpose.

God has a purpose FOR your pain, a reason for your struggle, and A REWARD for your faithfulness.

"Humble yourselves therefore under the mighty hand of God, that he may exalt you in due time: Casting all your care upon him; for he careth for you." (1Peter 5:6-7)

BONUS LESSON:

WHAT DO YOU DO WHEN YOU DO NOT KNOW WHAT TO DO?

2 Chronicles 20:12-20

Neither Know We What to Do

[12] " O our God, wilt thou not judge them? For we have no might against this great company that cometh against us; neither know we what to do, but our eyes are upon thee."

O our God... but our eyes are upon thee.

1. **Prayer**: Do not know what to do? The first thing do is prayer. Lots and lots of prayer until God reveals to you what to do.

[13] "And all Judah stood before the LORD, with their little ones, their wives, and their children. [15] And he said, Hearken ye, all Judah, and ye inhabitants of Jerusalem, and thou king Jehoshaphat, Thus saith the LORD unto you, Be not afraid nor dismayed by reason of this great multitude; for the battle is not yours, but God's."

Thus saith the LORD unto you

2. **Listen:** Do not know what to do? Make sure you are listening to the Lord. Pay attention when God speaks to you through the Bible, the Holy Spirit, your Church, and your Christian Friends.

"Be not afraid nor dismayed by reason of this great multitude; for the battle is not yours, but God's."

3. **Do not be afraid:** Do not know what to do? Do not be afraid or troubled. Do not allow yourself to be scared, because the struggle is not yours. You may feel you are alone in the middle of your troubles, but if you trust in God – He has got this.

   16 "To morrow go ye down against them...[17] Ye shall not need to fight in this battle: set yourselves,"

4. **Remain faithful:** Do not know what to do? Remain faithful to your God. Continue to be devoted to your Bible reading, daily prayer time, church attendance, and your good works to others. Determine to display your loyalty by setting yourself in the correct attitude towards God. Keep yourself thinking with a positive outlook to what God is and will be doing.

   "stand ye still and see the salvation of the LORD with you, O Judah and Jerusalem!' fear not, nor be dismayed; tomorrow go out against them, for the LORD will be with you."

5. **Stand Still:** Do not know what to do? Wait and see what God will do. Sometimes the best thing to do is doing nothing. Remain calm and do not panic. Do not make decisions based upon emotion. Just wait on your God. He has got this.

[18]" And Jehoshaphat bowed his head with his face to the ground, and all Judah and the inhabitants of Jerusalem fell before the LORD,"

6. **Humble yourself:** Do not know what to do? Do not allow yourself to dwell on yourself and your problems. Do not let your life be defined by everything that is happening to you. Humbly accept God's plan and purpose in your situation and do not allow pride to make you a victim.

"worshiping the LORD. [19] Then the Levites of the children of the Kohathites and of the children of the Korahites stood up to praise the LORD God of Israel with voices loud and high."

7. **Worship the Lord:** Do not know what to do? Praise and worship your God. He has blessed you before. He will continue to bless you. Count your blessing even the blessings you now have during your troubles. Praise your God for He is good to you and He loves you. He will never leave you or forsake you. Praise your God.

20 "And they rose early in the morning, and went forth into the wilderness of Tekoa: and as they went forth, Jehoshaphat stood and said, Hear me, O Judah, and ye inhabitants of Jerusalem; Believe in the LORD your God, so shall ye be established; believe his prophets, so shall ye prosper. 22 And when they began to sing and to praise, the LORD set ambushments against the children of Ammon, Moab, and mount Seir, which were come against Judah; and they were smitten."

And they rose early in the morning and went forth

8. **Follow the leading of the Lord.** Do not know what to do? Follow the leading of the Holy Spirit. He will speak to you leading you in a direction in your life. Do what is your are told to do. You never overcome your troubles and the fears that come with them without the leading of the Holy Spirit. Allow Him to lead you through this and then you shall overcome.

ONE LAST THING

Psalm 37:1-9

"Fret not thyself because of evildoers, neither be thou envious against the workers of iniquity. For they shall soon be cut down like the grass, and wither as the green herb."

- **FRET NOT:** Do not worry about those that do evil against you. They are not your concern for God will deal with them in due time.

- **ENVY NOT:** Do not concern yourself with how successful evil people seem to be. Do not wish you could be as care free as they are. God will deal with them in due time.

"Trust in the LORD, and do good; so shalt thou dwell in the land, and verily thou shalt be fed."

- **TRUST THE LORD:** Look to God for your only hope is in Him. And while it may seem to you the evil doers in this world are winning and are better off then you, your story is not over yet. God has never failed anyone who has placed their lives in His hands. We live by faith not by sight.

"Delight thyself also in the LORD; and he shall give thee the desires of thine heart."

- **DELIGHT THYSELF IN THE LORD:** Enjoy being a Christian. Enjoy going to church, reading the Bible, and enjoy your service for God. Enjoy all

God has given you. Remember the joy of the Lord is our strength.

"Commit thy way unto the LORD; trust also in him; and he shall bring it to pass. And he shall bring forth thy righteousness as the light, and thy judgment as the noonday."

- **COMMIT TO THE LORD:** Do not forsake the Lord just because you are going through some difficult times. Commit yourself to stay faithful to God, He has already committed to stay faithful to you. He in Hebrews 13:5 stated that He will never leave you nor forsake you. Can you state the same to Him?

"Rest in the LORD, and wait patiently for him: fret not thyself because of him who prospereth in his way, because of the man who bringeth wicked devices to pass."

- **REST AND WAIT ON THE LORD:** Calm down and know God is working on His timetable not your timetable. Wait for God's moment in your life.

"Cease from anger, and forsake wrath: fret not thyself in any wise to do evil. For evildoers shall be cut off: but those that wait upon the LORD, they shall inherit the earth."

- **CEASE FROM ANGER:** Stop being angry and blaming God. Stop being angry and blaming others. Stop being angry and blaming yourself. All your worry, blaming, and rage will not solve one little thing. Matter of fact it can only make things worse. Just wait on God to do His plan for your life. Trust Him, He knows what He is doing.

GOD LOVES YOU.
HIS PLAN FOR YOU IS DRIVEN BY THAT LOVE.

Do Not Listen To Your Negative Talk

"There is that speaketh like the piercings of a sword:but the tongue of the wise is health." (Proverbs 12:18)

This Proverb is so true when you apply it to self-talk. Many times, you are you worse critic cutting yourself to pieces. To be honest so much of your negative talk is a lie and listening to a lie is never healthy.

The truth is no one has ever negative talked themselves into a better life.

Listening to your negative talk will cause you to feel insignificant and incapable. The self-destructive lies you tell yourself will guarantee your struggle to accomplish God's purpose for your life. The truth is no one has ever negative talked themselves into a better life.

This lesson will help you identify nine hurtful negative talks to avoid in your life.

1. Your negative talk will tell you that you are not worth having friends.

Your negative talk will mislead you into some level of denial that you are not friendship material. People just want to use to you. Your negative talk will tell you compared to others you do not measure up to those that have lots of friends. But the truth is you can be a very valuable friend. The truth is your fear of rejection hinders you from friendship.

"A man that hath friends must shew himself friendly..." (Proverbs 18:24)

2. Your negative talk will tell you your bad behavior is alright - no one cares what you do.

Your negative talk tries to convince you that you can get away with anything because no one will ever care. No one really cares enough about you to care about what you do. The problem is you know your bad behavior and you cannot forget. This sets off a switch in your brain and dooms you to becoming an uncaring person yourself.

"By humility and the fear of the LORD are riches, and honour, and life." (Proverbs 22:4)

3. Your negative talk will tell you that you deserved the bad thing that happen to you.

Your negative talk wants you to forget how bad things were. You tell yourself to remember, "You are no angel" or "You did nothing to stop it." So eventually, you will have subtle thoughts that say "What happen was not really so bad." But of course, it was that bad. Which is why you are continually looking for help out of memories of what happen. Truth is no one deserves to have happen to them what happen to you. You need tell someone what happen. You need to tell your God.

"Bear ye one another's burdens, and so fulfil the law of Christ." (Galatians 6:2)

"Casting all your care upon him; for he careth for you." (1Peter 5:7)

4. Your negative talk will tell you that there is no one that understands you.

Your negative talk will tell you that no one in life really knows you or understands your problems. You will feel that you are on your own. The people have nothing to knowledge for you, "This is a nice advice, but it is not for me." Your negative talk will not allow yourself to grow and evolve as a person. Negative talk will not allow you to learn new things. In fact it wants you to stagnate in our growth so that you will revert back to what you know best - taking care of yourself. Your negative talk will hinder you from pushing yourself to keep growing as a person. Truth is you need people to challenge your selfish thoughts and harmful behaviors.

"Iron sharpeneth iron; so a man sharpeneth the countenance of his friend." (Proverbs 27:17)

5. Your negative talk will tell you to isolate yourself.

Your negative talk will tell you that being alone is your best chance of never being hurt. Because, you are vulnerable and it is better to be left to your own thinking. If you do not interact with others on a regular basis you forget the damage others have done to you. Truth is Isolation can be devastating to your personal growth. The subtle thoughts of how terrible life is and you want not part of it will build up over time and push you deeper into despair. The only way to get relief is to interact with others and discover that are some really good people in this life.

"Through desire a man, having separated himself, seeketh and intermeddleth with all wisdom. A fool hath no delight in understanding, but that his heart may discover itself." (Proverbs 18:1-2)

6. Your negative talk will tell you to resent others.

Your negative talk loves anger. And if you let our resentments run wild, completely unchecked, they will eventually get the better of you and drive you away from the people you love and loves you. Your anger will eventually over ride rational thought if you let it get out of control. The problem is not everyone else, the problem is you. Truth is forgiveness and love is the answer for a healthy life.

"And above all things have fervent charity among yourselves: for charity shall cover the multitude of

sins. Use hospitality one to another without grudging." (1Peter 4:8-9)

7. Your negative talk will tell you to feel sorry for yourself.

Your negative talk is in reality: selfish. So, self-pity is a favorite emotion of negative talk, because it is entirely self-centered and allows you to be lazy. What happens is that you start playing a victim role, feel sorry for yourself, and this justifies the idea that you do not have to take any action. You exempt yourself from doing something about the problems. Truth is you are a victim because you want to be a victim. God has a purpose and plan for your life and even your pain and hurt is a part of His plan. Accept His plan and purpose and you will stop being a victim.

"And we know that all things work together for good to them that love God, to them who are the called according to his purpose." (Romans 8:28)

8. Your negative talk will tell you are bored.

Your negative talk will tell you that you had a better life in your sin. After you have cleaned up your life for a while and conquered some of your most destructive sins; your negative talk will tell you that you were more fun when you were drinking, drugging, adultery, and being crazy. If you forget the lessons you have learned and stop growing or stop learning from God's Word then this is what will happen eventually. Truth is it was not that much fun. You forget how miserable your life was. Why would you want to return to that nasty life?

"As a dog returneth to his vomit, so a fool returneth to his folly." (Proverbs 26:11)

9. Your negative talk will tell you to live in fear.

Your negative talk ultimately wants you to live in fear, because that is when you will be most vulnerable. When fear is running your life, you will have a tendency to make poor decisions and possibly fall back on bad behavior that you feel will comfort your fear. Truth is you do not have to live in fear. Find a way to reach out others Christians and allow them to help you. Reach out to your God and allow His power and love strengthen you. If you can do this on a consistent basis then these fears that come from your negative talk dissolve.

"Fear thou not; for I am with thee: be not dismayed; for I am thy God: I will strengthen thee; yea, I will help thee; yea, I will uphold thee with the right hand of my righteousness." (Isaiah 41:10)

"For God hath not given us the spirit of fear; but of power, and of love, and of a sound mind." (2Timothy 1:7)

Your negative talk will drown out the truth. Instead, challenge your negative talk with the truth. Do not allow your negative talk to keep you stuck in an unhealthy life. A successful life awaits those who are directed by the truth.

Your negative talk is a liar and listening to a liar is never healthy. The Bible states that the Devil is a Liar. He is the father of lies.

"Ye are of your father the devil, and the lusts of your father ye will do. He was a murderer from the beginning, and abode not in the truth, because there is no truth in him. When he speaketh a lie, he speaketh of his own: for he is a liar, and the father of it." (John 8:44)

Reread the nine points of negative talk and replace negative talk with the Devil and you realize who is actually whispering in your ear.

NOW THIS IS THE END

ABOUT THE AUTHOR

MICHAEL WAYNE SNIDER

Michael Snider is a Pastor and has been preaching for thirty-nine years. He is a Certified Life coach, Certified Public Speaker and Lecturer, and a Certified Cognitive Behavioral Counselor. Michael has many years of working in the Social Service field. He has been a director of an addiction program for fourteen years. Michael is also the author of two books, *"Living By The Rule"* and *"Memoirs of a Dragon Slyer"*. Michael's lessons can be found on his blog, Livingbetternow.org and his sermons on his YouTube channel, Michael Wayne Snider.

www.ingramcontent.com/pod-product-compliance
Lightning Source LLC
LaVergne TN
LVHW010550100826
845148LV00013B/2688

* 9 7 8 1 7 3 5 1 4 5 4 9 5 *